The 48 Laws of Money

The Keys to Mastering Entrepreneurship, Networking, Leadership and Building Wealth

Ethan Clark

Only The Sovereign

Contents

Chapter One

Introduction

The world of business is more competitive than ever. If you want to make serious money, you can't just play the game - you need to dominate it. The old strategies won't cut it anymore. You have to be willing to innovate, take risks, and outwork everyone else.

Technology is changing everything at a rapid pace. Industries are transforming, markets are going global, and the lines between different fields are blurring. In this new landscape, the only way to succeed is to be adaptable, bold, and relentless in pursuing your goals.

Fortunes are being made and lost quicker than ever before. One smart move can change everything, but one mistake can cost you big time. If you want to thrive in this environment, you need to be on top of your game every single day.

So if you're serious about making it big in business, you need to embrace the grind. Study your industry inside and out, master the latest tools and strategies and never back down from a challenge. The competition may be fierce, but if you've got the drive and the discipline to push through, the rewards can be massive.

Why These 48 Laws Are Essential

The 48 Laws of Money isn't just another business book - it's a survival guide for the modern entrepreneur. These laws have been forged in the tough realities of today's business world, and they're designed to give you the strategies and mindset you need to succeed.

Each law is a lesson learned from the trenches. It's a manifesto for those who are willing to challenge the status quo and carve their own path to success. It's for the dreamers, the risk-takers, the ones who believe that they have what it takes to build something great.

These laws will challenge you to think differently about money, business, and your own potential. They'll push you out of your comfort zone and force you to confront the limiting beliefs that have been holding you back.

But if you're willing to embrace the challenge, the rewards can be incredible. By mastering these 48 laws, you'll gain the clarity, confidence, and control you need to navigate the complex world of business and come out on top.

Chapter Two

Build a Strong Foundation

Establishing a strong foundation is crucial for your business's long-term success. Think of these laws as the bedrock you build your empire on. Without a solid base, your business will be vulnerable to every market shift or challenge that comes your way.

Law 1: Start Cheap

Starting a business doesn't have to cost you. In fact, smart hustlers who know how to get things done without breaking the bank are the ones that come out on top.

Don't get it twisted, it's not about being cheap. It's about being strategic. In the ruthless world of business, you can't afford to blow your load on fancy offices and rental cars. That's a rookie move.

The name of the game is bootstrapping. Build your empire from the ground up, using what you have. Debt is a trap, don't fall for it.

In 2024, the internet is your best friend. With one viral post, you can be the king of your niche without spending a dime on billboards or TV ads.

Every dollar you save is ammo for your business. Be smart with your spending. Don't just throw money at a problem and hope it goes away. Spend with precision.

Here's a pro tip: Always validate your idea before going all in. Wanna sell t-shirts? Don't go printing 1000 of them just to watch them collect dust in your garage. Start small, test the market, see if people actually like your designs. If they do, **then** you ramp up production. If not, you pivot without losing your shirt (pun intended).

Being lean isn't about being small, it's about being agile. It's about striking hard and fast, making every move count. In the high-stakes game of business, the lean hustlers are the ones who come out on top.

So don't let anyone tell you that you need a million dollars to start a business. That's bullshit. All you need is a solid plan, a hustler's spirit and the smarts to make your money work for you. Keep your operations tight, your mind sharp, and your eyes on the prize. That's how you win in this game.

Law 2: Identify your strengths

In life, the hand you're dealt matters, but how you play it is what really counts. It's not just about knowing your strengths, it's about using them strategically. This is a game of chess, not checkers.

Understanding what you and your team are good at is crucial. Some people have a natural talent for communication, others are born strategists. If creativity isn't your strong suit, find someone who complements your skills. Let them handle the big ideas while you focus on execution.

Your team should be diverse, with each member bringing something unique to the table. From the charismatic negotiators to the cool-headed problem solvers, everyone has a role to play. The key is knowing how to leverage your team's strengths to exploit the market's weaknesses.

And don't forget, your weaknesses are just opportunities for someone else to shine. Outsourcing is a smart play. Focus on what you do best and delegate the rest.

At the end of the day, it's about assembling a team of talented individuals, each with their own area of expertise. It's about putting the right people in the right positions. And being the leader who orchestrates it all.

So take a hard look at yourself and your team. Identify what makes each of you unique, what gives you an edge. Then, use that knowledge to your advantage.

Law 3: Aim extremely high

Just aiming for success is for the weak. I talk to a lot of guys who say they want to make 10k a month. I get it, it's a solid milestone, but you're selling yourself short. Why not aim for $100k a month? Shoot for the stars and you'll at least land on the moon. And trust me, even if you "only" hit 10k a month, you'll be miles ahead of where you would've been with a smaller target.

Here's the thing: when you set your sights higher, everything changes. Your habits, your work ethic, the way you carry yourself - it all levels up. You'll find yourself more motivated, more energized. You'll start looking at your life differently.

Too many people are afraid to aim high because they don't want to fall short. But that's a loser's mentality. No boss ever got to the top by playing it safe. It's all about your mindset. If you're scared of setting big goals, it's probably because deep down, you know you'll have to step up your game drastically to reach them. You can't be lazy and hit $1M a month. You can't slack off and expect to be a millionaire.

But here's the beauty of it: even if you don't quite hit your crazy high target, you'll still end up achieving way more than you would have with a "realistic" goal. If you're aiming for $1M a month and you "only" make $100k, you're still killing it. But if your goal was 5k a month, you might hit it and then what? A couple of fancy dinners and you're back to square one.

Big goals force you to confront your weaknesses, your bad habits. They make you look inward and ask yourself what you need to change to reach the next level. And those changes stick with you, even if you don't quite reach your original target.

Small goals don't really change your life. But big goals? They can change everything, for you and the people you care about.

So don't be afraid to set goals that make you uncomfortable. Embrace that fear. Let it fuel you. Aim so high that people think you're crazy. Because at the end of the day, it's not about whether you hit the exact number. It's about how far you go, how much you grow, in pursuit of something extraordinary.

Law 4: Never waste time

Time is the one thing you can never get back, and in this game, every second counts.

The clock is always ticking and each moment is a chance to make things happen, to take another step towards your goals. The real hustlers understand that every minute wasted is an opportunity lost forever.

The second you truly grasp how precious time is, something changes inside you. You develop this insane drive, this need to make every moment count. You start moving with a sense of urgency, like every second could be your last chance to leave your mark on the world. And the truth is, it very well could be.

When you're chasing down your dreams, there's no room for hesitation or second-guessing. Hesitation is the birthplace of doubt, and doubt is the killer of action. It's a simple formula: move with purpose, with speed and with an unshakable belief that time is the most valuable resource you have. Once it's gone, it's gone for good.

You have to treat every day like it's your last, like it's your final opportunity to prove yourself. Wake up every morning ready to go to war for your dreams. Attack every task, every challenge with a sense of urgency. Don't wait for the "perfect moment" to make a move, because that moment doesn't exist. The only perfect moment is now.

Successful people don't have time for excuses or procrastination. They're too busy making moves, seizing opportunities and turning their vision into reality. They understand that life isn't going to wait for them to be ready. They have to be ready now, ready to strike while the iron is hot.

So if you want to make it in this world, if you want to achieve something truly great, you need to develop an almost obsessive relationship with time. Treat every second as a gift, an opportunity to push yourself closer to your goals. Don't waste a single moment on things that don't matter, on people who don't support your vision.

Remember, the clock is ticking. What are you going to do with the time you have left? Will you let it slip away, or will you seize it, own it, and use it to create the life you've always dreamed of? The choice is yours, but the clock is ticking. So make your move, and make it count.

Law 5: Protect your reputation

Your reputation is everything. But it's not about being loved by everyone - that's unrealistic. What matters is ensuring that respect outweighs disdain.

People don't trash talk you for no reason. Often, it's because they feel slighted or ignored. In business, you can't afford to turn a blind eye to discontent. One ignored complaint can spiral into a full-blown PR crisis. Address issues head-on to keep them manageable.

Every move you make shapes your reputation, so think before you act. Rash decisions can ruin you, while calculated ones build empires.

It's a balancing act. Too much fear and you'll be seen as a tyrant. Too much appeasement and you'll be viewed as weak. Strike the right chord between respect and healthy fear.

Guard your reputation fiercely. Handle mistakes swiftly and responsibly. Your name opens doors or slams them shut. Treat it like gold, because that's what it is in this world.

Chapter Three

Develop Key Business Skills

Mastering sales, marketing and market research is essential to monetizing your vision. Sales turns interest into income, marketing gets your product in front of the right people and market research ensures you understand your target audience. When you master this trio, you can turn any idea into a profitable venture. Continuously refine your approach based on data and feedback and there's no limit to what you can achieve.

Law 6: Develop persuasion skills

Persuasion is a critical skill in sales. It's not just about having a great product, but about communicating its value effectively.

To be persuasive, you need to speak with conviction and energy. Your words should draw people in and make them want to listen.

Remember, people don't just buy products, they buy the benefits those products provide. They buy the better version of themselves that your product can help them become.

To master persuasion, start by truly believing in what you're selling. Then, communicate that belief with passion and enthusiasm. Make your audience feel that your product is something they can't afford to miss out on.

At the end of the day, people buy from people they trust and believe in. Be that person.

Law 7: Know your product intimately

To excel in sales, you need to know your product inside and out. If you're unsure about your product's value, how can you expect potential customers to buy into it?

When you're pitching, even a moment of hesitation can kill the deal. It signals a lack of confidence and confidence is crucial in sales.

You have to be able to counter objections quickly and convincingly. Even the best product won't sell if you can't clearly articulate its value.

Simplicity is key. Can you distill your product's essence into something so compelling that it becomes irresistible?

It's not just about knowing your product's features, but also understanding who it's for. Who's your target market? Why does your product matter to them? What sets it apart from the competition? It's about connecting with your audience on a meaningful level.

When you're out there selling, remember: your product is more than just a set of features. It's a solution. It's a way to make someone's dream a reality. Know your product better than anyone else, and you won't just gain customers - you'll gain loyal advocates.

Live and breathe your product and the sales will follow.

Law 8: Constant outreach

If you want to make it big, you can't just sit back and wait for people to come to you. You gotta be out there, constantly pushing your brand, your product, your vision. You need to be everywhere your audience is looking. But this isn't about spamming people or posting random shit just to make noise. It's about being strategic, about making your presence felt in a way that can't be ignored.

You gotta know when to push hard and when to switch things up. When your competitors are quiet, that's when you need to be loud. When they're whispering, you need to be shouting. The goal is to make your brand not just visible, but unavoidable.

Rejection is just part of the game. Every "no" you hear is just bringing you one step closer to the "yes" that's going to change everything. You can't let it slow you down.

Your outreach needs to be relentless, but it also needs to be smart. It's about being everywhere at once, but also knowing how to be in the right place at the right time, in front of the right person. This isn't just about making people aware of your business, it's about making them feel like they need it, like they can't live without it.

You can't afford to hesitate. While you're sitting around thinking about your next move, your competitors are out there making moves. You need to seize every opportunity, use every platform, exploit every channel.

Don't just blast out the same message everywhere. Tailor your approach to each platform, each audience. What works on Instagram might not work on LinkedIn. What resonates with one group might fall flat with another. This is where your market research comes in - use what you know about your target audience to craft outreach that speaks directly to them.

And don't just think in terms of sales. Every interaction, every touchpoint, is a chance to build your brand, to create a connection. Whether it's a tweet, a blog post, or a face-to-face meeting, every communication should be leaving a lasting impression.

The goal isn't just to make a sale. It's to build a relationship, to create a loyal customer who will keep coming back and will tell their friends about you. That's how you build a real business, a lasting empire.

So don't hide in the shadows. Don't wait for the perfect moment. Get out there and make your presence known. Be the brand they can't escape, the product they can't stop thinking about, the vision they want to be a part of.

Law 9: Quality networking is crucial

Building a quality network isn't about collecting business cards or making small talk at boring industry events. It's about finding people who are just as driven and hungry for success as you are. When you do networking right, you're creating a team of allies, each with their own unique skills, who can help you reach levels of success you couldn't achieve on your own.

Imagine having a group of people who have your back, not just for the superficial stuff, but for the real, late-night conversations about your next big move. It's about connecting with people who get the vision, who understand the potential in every handshake and every conversation.

This isn't about aimless mingling. It's strategic alliance-building. It's about finding the key players who resonate with your hustle and your energy, the ones who can open doors for you when it counts. Quality networking is about understanding that your net worth is a reflection of your network. It's about being selective, purposeful and always aiming to give as much value as you get, if not more.

Seek out the people who are where you want to be - potential mentors, partners, even competitors. Their knowledge is invaluable. But don't just focus on what you can get from them. Make yourself so valuable that they want you in their corner. Before you ask for anything, offer something. Your unique insights, your energy, your willingness to go above and beyond - these are all things you can bring to the table.

In a world full of fakeness, being genuine is your secret weapon. The real players can spot a phony from a mile away. Be real, be yourself, but be your best self.

And stay open to the unexpected. Sometimes the most powerful connections come from surprising places. Stay sharp, stay authentic and stay ready.

Because ultimately, your network is a huge factor in your success. The people you surround yourself with, the alliances you build - these will form the foundation of your empire. So choose wisely, give generously and keep pushing forward. That's how you build a network that will help you reach the top.

Law 10: Analyze those more successful than you

If you want to rise to the top of your game, you need to start by studying the ones who are already there. Look at the heavy hitters in your industry. What moves did they make to get where they are? What risks did they take? But don't just focus on their highlights - pay close attention to where they stumbled, too. Every part of their journey is a lesson, a roadmap showing you what to do and what to avoid.

If you can, try to get some one-on-one time with these people. But remember, real mentorship isn't about putting them on a pedestal. It's about really digging into their story, understanding not just their wins, but also their losses. Because it's in those failures that you'll find the real gems of wisdom, the lessons that are hidden behind the temporary setbacks.

This kind of deep analysis is your secret weapon, your guide to getting to the top. Every single person you look up to was once a beginner, just like you. They all faced failures, learned from them and used those lessons to carve their own path to success.

But the goal isn't to just mimic these people. It's not about becoming a clone of your heroes. It's about soaking up their knowledge, breaking down their strategies, and then using that to fuel your own unique journey.

And don't just stop at one person. Look at a range of successful people, both in your industry and outside of it. The more perspectives you can learn from, the more tools you'll have in your arsenal.

Remember, success leaves clues. The ones at the top got there for a reason. It's your job to figure out what those reasons are and use them to fuel your own climb to greatness.

But through it all, never lose sight of what makes you unique. Your journey isn't about becoming someone else - it's about becoming the best version of yourself. So learn from the greats, but always stay true to who you are.

Chapter Four

Marketing and Sales Rules

In a world of dwindling attention spans, mastering marketing and sales is a must. Know your audience better than they know themselves. Speak to their desires, fears, and unspoken dreams. Craft messages that resonate deep within their souls. When you can connect with your audience on this level, selling becomes infinitely easier. Always provide value and position yourself as a trusted authority.

Law 11: Use social media

In the digital age, your online presence is everything. Having a big, engaged following on social media is like having a golden ticket. It's an asset that can open more doors and create more opportunities than any traditional investment.

When you build a strong social media, you're not just getting a bunch of followers. You're creating a whole market of potential customers, a community of people who might want to work with you, and a stage to show off what you're all about. It doesn't matter if you're an OnlyFans baddie, a dude slinging t-shirts, a fitness guru, or a kitchen knife hustler. Social media gives you a direct line to the people who are most likely to buy what you're selling.

And let's talk about bang for your buck. Social media marketing blows traditional methods out of the water. Why waste time and money handing out flyers when you can hit thousands, even millions, with one targeted ad? Got a product to push? Pay an influencer to hype it up and watch your reach skyrocket. You're tapping into their followers to boost your own.

But it's not just about business. A strong social media presence can level up your whole life. Dating, networking, finding people to collaborate with, even hunting for top-tier talent to join your team. Your clout on socials can be the key that unlocks it all. Forget a boring ass resume, a killer Instagram profile can land you the job of your dreams.

So if you're not taking social media seriously, you're missing out on a major key to success. It's not just a place to post pretty pictures and funny memes. It's a tool, a weapon in your arsenal. Master it, and watch your life change.

But it's not just about the flex. A strong social media presence shows the world that you're somebody to pay attention to. It's proof that you've got something to say, something to offer. It's a way to build trust, credibility, and a loyal following that will be with you for the long haul.

Law 12: Create urgency

To turn a "maybe" into a "hell yes", you gotta make your customers feel the heat. They need to feel like if they don't act now, they're gonna miss out on something big. But this isn't about backing them into a corner. It's about showing them why now is the time to make a move.

Think about Black Friday. People go apeshit for those deals. Why? Because of the urgency, the fear of missing out on a bargain. That's the kind of energy you want to tap into. But be careful. If you overdo it, the magic fades. You don't want your brand to come off like a cheap discount store.

Creating urgency is about more than just pushing sales. It's about really understanding what your customers need on a deep level. It's about showing them how waiting could mean missing out on something that could change their lives. This isn't about manipulation. It's about motivation. Your product isn't just another thing to buy. It's the key to unlocking their full potential.

Remember, the goal isn't to pressure people. It's to persuade them. You want to make the idea of not buying more painful than handing over their credit card. Because at the end of the day, urgency is all about value. It's about making your customers realize that what you're offering right now is too good to pass up.

So when you're crafting your pitch, always keep urgency in mind. Make every offer feel like a once-in-a-lifetime chance. Show your customers why they need to act now, not later.

But remember, urgency without substance is just hype. You gotta back it up with real value. If your product doesn't live up to the urgent promise, you'll burn bridges instead of building loyalty.

So use urgency wisely. Use it to highlight the true worth of what you're offering. Use it to light a fire under your customers' asses and get them to take action. But always, **always** make sure you're delivering on what you promise. That's how you create urgency that leads to lasting success.

Law 13: Sell the problem

If you want to sell something, you can't just focus on what your product does. You gotta focus on the problems it solves. Whether you're pushing the latest high-tech gadget or a simple everyday item, your job is to shine a light on the issues your target audience is facing. You gotta point out problems they might not even realize they have. It's like holding up a mirror that shows them not just their current struggles, but the potential solution that your product offers.

Let's say you're selling a pen. You could talk about how it feels in your hand or how long the ink lasts, but that's not gonna hook people. Instead, you talk about the frustration of not being able to jot down a great idea before it slips away. You paint a picture of all the brilliant thoughts that get lost because they didn't have the right tool to capture them. Suddenly, your pen isn't just something to write with. It's a key to unlocking their creativity, to making sure their best ideas don't get lost in the shuffle.

Or maybe you're marketing a fitness program. You could list off the number of workouts or brag about your trainers' credentials, but that's not what's gonna get people to buy. What will, is tapping into that deep dissatisfaction they feel when they look in the mirror, that lack of confidence that comes from not feeling fit. You show them how your program isn't just a set of videos. It's a transformation, a path to becoming the best version of themselves.

This kind of selling isn't about features and specs. It's about understanding what makes people tick. You gotta get inside the heads of your potential customers, feel their pain points, and then speak directly to those issues. Your message has to hit them in the feels, make them feel like you get them, like you know exactly what they're going through. And most importantly, you gotta make them believe that with your product, they can make a change.

But this isn't about manipulating people. It's about connecting with them on a real, human level. It's about showing genuine empathy and offering a genuine solution. Because when you can do that, when you can make your audience feel seen and understood, that's when you create real brand loyalty.

So don't just sell your product. Sell the problem it solves. Paint a vivid picture of the struggles your audience faces and then show them how your offering is the answer they've been looking for. Do that, and you won't just make a sale. You'll make a customer for life.

Law 14: Satisfy immediate needs

To convince someone to buy what you're selling, you gotta focus on what they need right now, not what they might need later. It's all about the present, the immediate. That's the key to getting people to take action. They don't give a shit about how your product might help them a year from now if it doesn't solve their problems today.

Here's how you make this work:

1. **Focus on the now:** Make it crystal clear how what you're offering solves a problem they're facing right this second.

2. **Create urgency:** Make them feel like if they don't act now, they're gonna miss out or keep struggling with the same old issues.

3. **Immediate solutions:** Give them answers that they can use and benefit from quickly. They don't want to hear about results that might happen months or years down the line.

When you make your pitch all about their current situation, about the issues they're dealing with right here and now, saying yes to what you're offering becomes a no-brainer.

In a world where attention spans are shorter than ever and people want their needs met yesterday, being able to provide quick solutions isn't just a bonus - it's a must.

So don't get caught up trying to sell people on a far-off future. Focus on the present, on the problems they're facing today. Show them how you can make their life better, easier, or more enjoyable right now. That's how you get them to pull the trigger.

But remember, this isn't about making false promises. It's about really understanding what your audience needs and delivering on that need fast. It's about proving that you get them and that you've got the answer they've been looking for.

So dig deep, figure out what's keeping your potential customers up at night, and then show up with a solution that they can't ignore.

Law 15: Polarize for Profits

In order to make real money, you can't be afraid to stir shit up. The brands that really make a mark are the ones that aren't afraid to draw a line in the sand. It's simple: if you want people to remember you, you gotta get their attention first. And nothing grabs attention like a brand that's willing to stand for something, even if it pisses some people off.

Now, this doesn't mean being a dick just for the sake of it. It's about having the balls to stand up for what you believe in. Let your brand be a magnet for the people who align with your values and a repellant to the ones who don't.

Sure, courting controversy comes with some risks, but it's also where the big payoffs are. Every hater, every critic, is just throwing gasoline on the fire of your brand's visibility. There's a saying, "There's no such thing as bad publicity." In the age of social media, that's more true than ever. Every tweet, every comment, every share, whether it's from a fan or a hater, it all makes your brand harder to ignore. It's like they're all working for you, even when they're trying to tear you down.

So let the haters hate. They don't realize it, but they're actually helping build your empire. Every time they talk, they're laying another brick in the foundation of your success. They're making it so that your brand isn't just seen, it's impossible to miss.

Remember: if you try to please everyone, you'll end up being forgotten. If you want to be loved, you gotta be willing to be hated. You gotta be ready to polarize.

The brands that really kill it are the ones that know who they are and aren't afraid to show it. They're the ones that stand out in a sea of sameness. And yeah, that means some people aren't going to like you. But the ones who do, will love you. They'll be ride or die. And that's worth way more than being bland and inoffensive.

So don't be afraid to be bold. Don't be afraid to ruffle some feathers. Stand up for what you believe in, even if it means making some enemies. Controversy sells. Polarization pays. That's just how it is.

Law 16: Analyze why customers buy from you

Figuring out why your customers choose you over the competition isn't just interesting - it's your secret weapon. If one person buys for a specific reason, chances are there's a whole bunch of people out there who feel the same way. Your mission? Find that reason and make it the centerpiece of your marketing.

Getting to the bottom of the 'why' is like having a direct line to your customers' brains. Sold some merch? Hit them up. Ask what made them pull the trigger. Was it the design, the color, the message? This isn't about stroking your ego - it's about gathering intel. When you understand what makes people buy, you can double down on it.

This is all about laser-focused targeting. Crafting your marketing messages so tightly around the 'why' that your target audience can't help but see your product as the solution they've been dreaming of.

Forget throwing spaghetti at the wall and seeing what sticks. Being specific is your secret sauce. Speak directly to the people who have already shown they're down to buy what you're selling. Your current customers are a treasure trove of insight into your future ones. When you get what makes them tick, you're not just guessing who your target audience is - you know them inside and out.

So take the time. Ask the question. "Why did you choose me?" The answers might surprise you, but more importantly, they'll show you the way. Everyone's always talking about the 'how', 'where', and 'when', but the 'why' is often the most powerful piece of the puzzle.

Law 17: Make customers feel important

If you want to build a brand that people keep coming back to, you gotta make your customers feel like they're the most important people in the world. Imagine walking into a spot where everyone knows your name, knows what you like, and treats you like a king. That's the kind of experience we're trying to create with every single sale.

Here's how you do it:

Personal Touch: Every time you interact with a customer, make them feel like they're the only person that matters. Send them a personalized thank you note, hook them up with a birthday discount, or follow up to make sure they're happy with what they bought. These little things add up to a big difference.

Exclusive Experiences: Give your customers something they can't get anywhere else. Maybe it's first dibs on new products, VIP customer service, or an invite to an exclusive event. Make them feel like they're part of a special club and they'll rep your brand like it's their job.

Emotional Resonance: Connect with your customers on a real level by understanding what makes them tick. Match your brand values with their personal beliefs and they'll see your product as a part of who they are.

Feedback Loop: Show your customers that their opinions count. Actively ask for their feedback, and let them see how their input has shaped your business. This back-and-forth builds trust and makes customers feel like they're a part of your brand's story.

When customers feel important, they don't just come back - they become your biggest fans. This isn't about playing with emotions; it's about creating real connections. This approach doesn't just keep people coming back; it turns customers into a loyal community that can't wait to spread the word about a brand that makes them feel valued.

So don't just treat your customers like another number. Treat them like the VIPs they are. Show them that they matter to you, and they'll show you the kind of loyalty that money can't buy.

Law 18: Supply where there is demand

You might think you need to come up with the next groundbreaking idea to make it big. But let's be real - you don't need to reinvent the wheel. Just take a look around. The market is full of opportunities just waiting for someone to grab them. It's not about pulling something out of your ass. It's about seeing where the demand is and stepping up to meet it.

Think about all the personal trainers, online book sellers, sports clothing brands, and ski equipment companies out there. What's their big secret? It's simple. They saw a need and they filled it. They noticed people wanted something and they gave it to them. That's what business smarts are all about - being able to spot the opportunities, copy what works, and put your own spin on it.

Here's the game plan: Find a niche that's working, study the top dogs and learn from them. What are they doing right? Do that. Where are they dropping the ball? Don't make those same mistakes.

Forget all the talk about saturated markets. That's just a bullshit excuse from people who haven't figured out how to make it work. No market is too crowded for someone who's bringing real value, quality, and innovation to the table. If there's a market, there's a chance to dominate it. Your job is to carve out your own space, make your presence known and show that when you've got the right approach, there's always room for a new player.

So don't waste your time trying to come up with something completely new. Instead, look for the opportunities that are already out there. Find the niches where people are spending money and figure out how you can do it better. Study your competition, learn from their wins and losses and then put your own unique spin on it.

Remember, the money is where the demand is. So don't try to create demand out of nothing. Find where it already exists and focus on supplying it in a way that sets you apart.

Law 19: Don't appear desperate or needy

Even if your bank account is emptier than a politician's promise and the next sale is the only thing standing between you and living on the streets, you gotta keep your cool.

You need to adopt an abundance mentality. The world's wealth isn't some stagnant puddle - it's a constantly flowing river, and there's always more where that came from. This isn't about bluffing your way through negotiations with a poker face. It's about genuinely knowing your worth and believing in the value of what you're bringing to the table.

When you carry yourself with the confidence of someone who has options, you're not just another salesperson - you're a partner they want to work with. Desperation makes you forgettable, just another face in the crowd. But confidence? That makes you stand out. Remember, people aren't just buying your product - they're buying into the confidence you have in it.

So stand tall, even when every fiber of your being wants to crumble. Hold your head high, even when your bank balance is lower than your shoe size.

This principle applies to every aspect of life. Neediness pushes people away, but abundance draws them in. Whether you're trying to land a partnership or close a deal, the trick is to show them how much they need what you've got, not how much you need them. In a world with endless options, why should they choose you? Because you're not just another choice - you're the only choice that matters.

So don't let them see you sweat. Don't let them smell your fear. Carry yourself with the unshakable confidence of someone who knows their value and isn't afraid to own it. When you believe in yourself and your offering, others will too.

Chapter Five

Team Building and Management

Assembling and directing a team of sharp, driven individuals is crucial. Building and managing a team is more than just filling positions; it's about creating a cohesive unit that shares your vision, propels your goals and amplifies your success. This section explores the strategies and philosophies that transform a group of individuals into a powerful force, united in purpose and unrivaled in execution.

Law 20: Loyalty is key

When you're building your team, skills and experience are important. But there's one thing that trumps all of that: loyalty. You can teach someone new skills, you can help them improve their techniques, but loyalty? That's something you either have or you don't.

The smart play is to focus on building a team of ride-or-die loyalists.

Treat your inner circle like gold and they'll protect your business like it's their own. This isn't just about giving them a job - it's about creating a bond. It's about turning coworkers into soldiers who are ready to go to war for your vision.

It might sound harsh, but it's true: A skilled snake can bring your whole operation down, but a loyal soldier will have your back through thick and thin. In the cutthroat world of business, it's the loyal ones who give you real strength.

So don't just focus on resumes and qualifications. Look for people who believe in what you're doing, who are ready to bleed for the cause. Treat them right, give them a reason to be loyal and they'll be the foundation that your empire is built on.

Law 21: Fix problems quickly

In business, shit happens. It's not a matter of if, but when. And when those problems pop up, how quickly you handle them can be the difference between winning and losing. Issues like payment system glitches or dropping engagement aren't just going to fix themselves. You gotta jump on them fast and hard.

Find the problem, face it head-on and fix it. No bullshit, no delay. Sales slowing down? Change up your strategy **NOW**. Issues with your staff? Deal with it directly and get to the bottom of it ASAP. This isn't just about putting out fires - it's about turning those problems into opportunities to come back stronger and better.

When you handle issues quickly, you don't just stop them from getting worse. You actually push your business forward. You get smarter, tougher and better at what you do. It's not about the problems you face - it's about how fast and how hard you tackle them.

So don't be afraid of problems. Expect them. Be ready for them. And when they show up, don't flinch. Hit them head-on with everything you've got. The faster you solve them, the stronger you'll become.

Remember, in this game, speed is key. The quicker you are to identify and solve problems, the smoother your operation will run. And a smooth operation is a profitable operation.

So stay alert, stay proactive and always be ready to fight.

Law 22: Make money or save time

Every single person on your team needs to either be making you money or saving you time. It's that simple. Black and white. The value of a team member isn't just about getting their tasks done - it's about how they're impacting your bottom line or how they're making your operation more efficient.

A sales rep who's crushing their targets and bringing in big bucks is just as valuable as an assistant who's clearing your schedule so you can focus on the big moves. It's basic math - measure what they're doing, evaluate their impact, and make the call. You should be able to see clear as day how each person on your team is contributing. If they're not adding to your revenue or freeing up your time, they're dead weight. And in a game where speed and results are everything, you can't afford to carry any extra baggage.

You gotta look at your team with a magnifying glass. Every dollar you spend on a team member needs to be giving you a clear return, whether that's in minutes saved or money made. This isn't about being cold - it's about being strategic.

Now, this doesn't mean you need to create some kind of shark tank where everyone's out for themselves. It's about building a team of all-stars who are all working towards the same goal of being efficient and growing the business. When you think like this, you're not just making the most of what you've got - you're creating a powerhouse of a team that can take on anything that comes your way.

So don't be afraid to hold your team to a high standard.

Law 23: Hire family and friends

As mentioned earlier trust is everything. It's the secret sauce that keeps everything together. And who do you trust more than your day ones, your family and friends?

Think about it - the road to success is never smooth. There's always gonna be ups and downs. And when shit gets rough, who do you want in your corner? The people who've been there for your highest highs and your lowest lows.

When you work with family and friends, it's not just business anymore. It's a mission, a quest that you're all in together. It's about creating a team where everyone has a key role to play, not just because of what they can do, but because of the unbreakable bond you all share. This isn't about hooking your people up with jobs they don't deserve. It's about recognizing the unique skills and strengths they bring to the table and using them to push towards a common goal.

Now, some people might warn you about mixing business with pleasure. They'll say it's too risky, that it can mess up your personal relationships. But they're missing the point. This isn't about giving out free rides. It's about building a team of people you can trust with your life, people who will ride with you through the good times and the bad.

And when the challenges come (and they always do), these are the relationships that will give you the strength to keep pushing. Because you know you're not in it alone. You're all fighting for something bigger than yourselves.

Every great empire was built on a foundation of trust and loyalty. And there's no stronger foundation than the one you have with your family and friends. So don't be afraid to bring them into the business. Build your team with the people you trust most and watch as you all rise together.

Just remember, this isn't about handouts. It's about recognizing strength, harnessing loyalty and creating a unit that's unbreakable.

Law 24: Don't take things personally

In business, you gotta leave your feelings at the door. It's all about logic and strategy, not emotions. And trust me, there will be times when people let you down or straight up stab you in the back. But when that happens, you can't react with your heart. You gotta think with your head.

Cutting off snakes isn't about holding a grudge. It's about protecting your empire and the people who are loyal to you. It's not personal, it's just good business.

You have to be your own harshest critic, always pushing yourself to be better. At the end of every day, ask yourself: did I give it my all today? If the answer is no, then you need to step it up immediately. You don't have time to dwell on personal shit. Every second counts.

Like Michael Corleone said: "It's not personal, it's strictly business." That's the mindset you need to have.

Now, this doesn't mean you ignore all feedback. It means you consider the source and the intention behind it. If it's coming from your trusted inner circle or from experts in your field, then you should definitely take it into consideration. But if it's just haters trying to bring you down, tune it out. Not all criticism is constructive. Some people just want to see you fail.

At the end of the day, you can't let your emotions cloud your judgment. You gotta stay focused on the goal, no matter what. Betrayal, disappointment, haters - these are all just obstacles on the path to success. You gotta learn to navigate them with a cool head and a strategic mind.

Remember, in this game, it's the ones who can separate their feelings from their actions who come out on top. It's not about being heartless - it's about being smart. It's about knowing when to cut ties, when to push harder and when to ignore the noise.

So keep your eyes on the prize and don't let anyone or anything throw you off your game. Stay calculated, stay focused, and always, always keep it business. That's how you win.

Chapter Six

Finance and Growth

This section is all about the financial tactics and strategies you need to take your business to the next level.

Law 25: Get legal after getting rich

When you're just starting out, don't get bogged down with all the legalities. I'm not saying to do anything shady, but you don't need to be drowning in paperwork before you've even made a sale. Your priority should be getting your business off the ground and money coming in. The legal stuff can wait until you've got some cash in the bank.

I've seen too many people get so caught up in getting their EIN, VAT numbers and tax forms sorted that they never actually get around to launching their business. That's a rookie mistake. Your focus should be on getting out there, making sales, and generating revenue. Once you've got a proven business model and some profits to show for it, then you can bring in the lawyers.

Remember, action is what counts, not paperwork. Don't let the legal side of things distract you from your main goal: making money. Stack your cash first, then worry about dotting the i's and crossing the t's.

The last thing you want is to be drowning in legal fees before you've even had a chance to get your business off the ground. So keep it simple, keep it focused, and keep your eye on the prize. Get rich first, then get legal. That's the smart way to play the game.

Law 26: Charge higher prices

Charging premium prices is a way of telling the world that what you're offering is top-notch, cream of the crop, the best of the best.

It's not about being greedy, it's about setting the stage for your business to deliver an experience that's above and beyond. When you charge more, you're creating an aura of exclusivity and quality around your brand. You're telling your customers that they're not just buying a product or service, they're buying into a lifestyle, a status symbol.

By setting those high prices, you're attracting a different kind of clientele. These are the people who appreciate the finer things in life, who are willing to pay top dollar for the best. And by catering to that crowd, you're elevating your business to a whole new level.

See, while everyone else is racing to the bottom, slashing prices and competing for the bargain hunters, you're playing a different game. You're building a brand that's synonymous with luxury, with quality, with prestige. And that's how you win in the long run.

When you refuse to compromise on price, you're sending a message. You're telling the world that you believe in the value of what you're offering and you're not afraid to put a premium price tag on it. Each sale, each transaction, is a testament to the excellence of your brand.

But this isn't just about making money. It's about making a name for yourself. It's about building a legacy of quality and distinction that will outlast any temporary fluctuations in the market. It's about being the best and having the prices to match.

So don't be afraid to charge what you're worth. Don't get sucked into the race to the bottom. Stand tall, stand proud and let your prices reflect the unparalleled value you bring to the table.

Law 27: Take profits

Nothing in this world lasts forever, and that includes your business. No matter how untouchable you think you are, time is gonna catch up eventually. This isn't about being negative, it's about being smart and securing your bag while you can.

Too many young hustlers out here think they're building something that's gonna last forever. But the OGs know better. They know that when opportunity knocks, you gotta answer and get paid while the getting's good. The game is full of stories about big shots who thought they were invincible, only to end up broke because they didn't put their own money first.

So let me break it down: your business is just a way to stack cash, nothing more. It's a tool, not the end goal. You're not here to build some kind of monument to your greatness, you're here to fill your pockets so that when things inevitably hits the fan, you're not left holding the bag.

Think of your business like a temporary partnership with lady luck. Milk it for all it's worth, but always keep one eye on the door. Reinvest some of your profits, sure, but never forget that at the end of the day, this is about YOU getting paid. Because the ones who don't secure their own bag are always the first to get wiped out when the game changes.

So don't get it twisted. Stack your chips, secure your wealth and always be ready to cash out when the time is right. That's how you play this game and come out on top. The goal isn't to build something that lasts forever, it's to get rich and stay rich, no matter what happens to your business.

Remember, loyalty is great, but loyalty to your own financial future should always come first.

Law 28: Beat inflation

Alright, let's talk about the silent killer: inflation. Slowly but surely eating away at the value of every dollar you bust your ass to earn. But the good news is, the solution isn't rocket science. If you want to beat inflation at its own game, you gotta focus on three things: boosting your income, giving a middle finger to the bank and spreading your money across a bunch of different investments.

Now, when I say invest, I'm not just talking about throwing your cash into stocks and hoping for the best. Nah, I'm talking about investing in yourself, in your skills, in your reputation. You gotta make your money work for you, whether that's in crypto, real estate, stocks, or whatever else you're into. The key is to keep your money moving, to keep it active, because the moment you let it sit still, inflation starts taking big bites out of it.

See, inflation isn't something you can just ignore and hope it goes away. You gotta take the fight to it, and one of the best ways to do that is by raising your prices. Now, I know what you're thinking, "But won't that scare off my customers?" No. If you're delivering real value, if you're staying ahead of the game, your customers will understand. Raising prices isn't just about protecting your bottom line, it's about pushing yourself to be better, to justify that extra cost with even more services and products.

But the most powerful investment you can make is in yourself. Building skills that make you invaluable, about connecting with the right people, about staying on top of what's happening in the world. When you invest in yourself, you're creating a foundation for success that can weather any storm, even when the economy is taking a shit.

So yeah, inflation is a bitch, but it doesn't have to be your master. By focusing on increasing your income, diversifying your investments, and constantly leveling up your own game, you can stay ahead of the curve and keep your money growing, no matter what the market is doing.

Remember, this is a hustle and in the hustle, you can't afford to be passive. You gotta be proactive, you gotta be strategic and most of all, you gotta bet on yourself. Because at the end of the day, that's the investment that always pays off. So keep your head up, keep your money moving and keep pushing forward. Inflation can't touch you if you're always two steps ahead.

Law 29: Money coming in, is the business

Let's get down to what really matters: money coming in. You can have all the fancy branding, the slick website, the impressive office space - but if you have no cash flow, you have no business.

Too many people get caught up in the details, the window dressing. They think that if they get everything perfect on the surface, the money will just start rolling in. But that's ass-backwards. The real key to building a successful business is to focus on revenue from day one.

Think about it like this: when you're starting out, what's more important - having a perfect logo, or having paying customers? I'll tell you right now, it's the customers every time. Because customers bring in cash and cash is what keeps your business alive.

So how do you make sure you're prioritizing revenue? It's simple. Every decision you make, every strategy you employ, should be focused on one thing: bringing in more money. Whether that's through sales, marketing, partnerships - whatever it takes to get that cash flowing.

Now, I'm not saying the other stuff doesn't matter at all. Of course, you want to have a professional image, a strong brand. But those things should be in service of your revenue goals, not the other way around.

Think of it like building a house. You can have the most beautiful paint job, the most stylish furniture - but if you don't have a solid foundation, that house is gonna crumble. In business, revenue is your foundation. It's what everything else is built on.

So don't get distracted by the shiny objects, the vanity metrics.

Remember, at the end of the day, businesses exist to make money. It's not about having the coolest office or the most impressive business cards. It's about generating cash, plain and simple. Master that, and you'll be well on your way to building a real, sustainable business.

Chapter Seven

Competitive Advantage

In this section, we'll explore the strategies and mindsets that will give you a powerful competitive advantage in business. Get ready to learn how to give yourself an unfair edge in the cutthroat world of entrepreneurship.

Law 30: Speed is everything

In this game, speed is everything. If you aren't moving fast, you're falling behind. And I'm not just talking about how quickly you can get your product out there - I'm talking about speed in every aspect of your business. Making decisions, pivoting when you need to, responding to feedback - the faster you can do these things, the more shots you have at success.

Think about it like this: every time you make a move, you're creating an opportunity to learn, to grow, to evolve. The quicker you can make those moves, the more opportunities you create for yourself. It's like compounding interest for your business.

Let's say you're starting a new venture. If you take your sweet time, overthinking every little detail, you're missing out on valuable feedback from the real world. But if you move fast, get your product out there, start making sales - now you've got data to work with. You can see what's resonating with customers, what's falling flat and you can adapt accordingly. That's how you keep your momentum going, how you stay ahead of the curve.

There's a saying that sums this up perfectly: "Do more, think less." As an entrepreneur, you can't afford to get stuck in your own head. You gotta prioritize action over everything else. Because the more actions you take, the more chances you have to stumble onto something great.

Now, this doesn't mean you should just be reckless. You still need to be strategic, to think things through. But you can't let that thinking paralyze you. You gotta find the balance between planning and doing and then lean hard into the doing.

When you embrace this mindset of rapid execution, you're not just outmaneuvering your competitors - you're unlocking a whole new level of agility for your business. You're able to seize opportunities that others might miss because they're too slow to act.

Remember, the game favors the swift. So don't get bogged down in the details, don't let perfect be the enemy of good. Keep your foot on the gas, keep pushing forward and trust that your speed will take you where you need to go. In business, as in life, fortune favors the bold - and the fast.

Law 31: Upsell existing customers

When it comes to growing your business, there's no better strategy than upselling to your existing customers. These are the people who already know and trust you, who've already bought into what you're selling. They're your low-hanging fruit, your bread and butter.

Think about it - you've already put in the work to win them over that first time. You've built that relationship, established that trust. So when you go back to them with another offer, they're way more likely to say yes than some random person off the street. It's just human nature.

And here's the beautiful thing - not only is it easier to sell to existing customers, it's also a whole lot cheaper. You don't have to spend a ton of money on marketing and advertising to reach them. They're already in your orbit, ready and waiting for your next move.

But it's not just about the money you save - it's about the money you can make. When you turn a one-time customer into a repeat buyer, you're not just increasing your revenue - you're building a loyal fan base. And there's nothing more powerful for a business than word-of-mouth marketing from satisfied customers.

These are the people who are gonna sing your praises to their friends, their family, their coworkers. They're gonna be your unofficial brand ambassadors, spreading the gospel of your awesomeness far and wide. And that kind of organic growth is priceless.

But here's the key - none of this works if you don't prioritize quality in every single sale. You can't just slap together some half-assed product and expect people to come back for more. You gotta bring your A-game every time, deliver an experience that leaves them thrilled and eager for more.

So don't sleep on the power of upselling. It's not just a tactic - it's a cornerstone of sustainable growth. Treat your customers like gold, give them every reason to keep coming back, and watch as your business flourishes.

Law 32: Never say no to money

If there's one rule you never, ever break in business, it's this: never say no to money. I don't care what form it comes in - if someone's trying to give you cash, you take it. Period.

Now, I know what some of you are thinking. "But isn't that greedy? Shouldn't I have standards?" No. This isn't about greed, it's about recognizing opportunity. Today, money can come from all kinds of places, in all kinds of ways. Your job is to be ready to catch it, no matter what.

Maybe it's accepting payment in Bitcoin or Ethereum. Maybe it's bartering your services for something valuable in return. Maybe it's using some new app or platform to make transactions easier. The point is, you gotta be flexible. You gotta be open to different possibilities.

Think about it from your customer's perspective. The easier you make it for them to give you their money, the more likely they are to do it. If you're turning them away because you don't like their payment method, you're not just losing that sale - you're losing all the future sales that customer might have made.

But when you say yes, when you find a way to make it work, you're opening the floodgates. You're creating a stream of revenue that can keep flowing, keep growing, with every satisfied customer.

And here's the thing - sometimes the most lucrative opportunities come from the most unexpected places. If you're too rigid in how you think about money, you might miss out on a major windfall. But if you're open to the possibilities, if you're ready to seize every chance to grow your wealth, you might just stumble into the kind of success you never saw coming.

So don't get hung up on the details. Don't let your preconceptions about what "real" money looks like hold you back. Embrace the diversity of value in this new economy. Be ready to accept payment in any form, from anyone who's willing to give it.

Law 33: Be anti-fragile

Being anti-fragile is about creating a business model that gets stronger in the face of chaos, that uses disruption as fuel for growth.

Today, things can change overnight. New laws get passed, markets shift, technology evolves - and if you're not ready to roll with those punches, you're gonna get knocked out. But if you build anti-fragility into your business from the ground up, you'll be able to pivot, adapt, and come out on top no matter what gets thrown your way.

So how do you do it? First, you gotta diversify your income streams. You can't rely on just one product, one service, one market. That's like putting all your eggs in one basket - if something happens to that basket, you're screwed. Instead, you need to have multiple revenue channels, so if one takes a hit, the others can keep you afloat and even help you grow.

Next, you gotta be flexible with how you get paid as we said. We're living in a digital age and if you're still stuck on just cash and checks, you're limiting yourself. Embrace all the options - credit cards, online payments, crypto, even good old-fashioned bartering. The more ways you can accept payment, the more customers you can serve, and the less vulnerable you are to any single payment method going down.

Another key move? Spread your money around. Don't just stick with one bank, one institution. Because if that one place hits a snag, your whole operation could be in jeopardy. By using multiple banks, you're protecting yourself from being taken down by any one entity's mistakes or malice.

And when it comes to getting the word out, don't do all your marketing in one place. You gotta be everywhere - social media, email, blogs, podcasts, you name it. That way, if one platform changes their algorithm or kicks you off, you still have a direct line to your audience.

But here's the most important thing: all of this is about being resourceful, adaptable, and resilient. It's about having a business that can take a hit and come back swinging. It's about being able to turn obstacles into opportunities, to use the chaos of the world as a launching pad for growth.

Law 34: Break the rules when needed

I know this might sound counterintuitive, but hear me out. Sometimes, the path to success, to game-changing innovation, lies outside the lines that everyone else is coloring inside.

Now, I'm not saying you should go out and start breaking laws. That's not what this is about. It's about knowing when the rules are holding you back, when they're keeping you from reaching your full potential. It's about having the guts to challenge the status quo, to look at the way things have always been done and say, "There's gotta be a better way."

Think about all the entrepreneurs who have really made their mark, who have disrupted entire industries and built empires. They didn't get there by following the same old playbook as everyone else. They got there by taking risks, by pushing boundaries, by daring to do what others said couldn't be done.

Breaking the rules isn't about being reckless or unethical. It's about being strategic, about knowing which rules are meant to be bent and which ones are meant to be shattered. It's about understanding the difference between what's truly impossible and what's just never been attempted.

In a lot of ways, this ties back to the idea of anti-fragility that we talked about before. When you're willing to break the mold, to adapt and innovate in the face of obstacles, you're building a business that can thrive in chaos. You're creating something that's not just resilient, but anti-fragile - something that actually gets stronger when it's tested.

But I'm not gonna lie to you - this path isn't for everyone. It takes a certain kind of person to look at the rules and say, "Thanks, but no thanks." It takes courage, it takes vision, and it takes a whole lot of hustle. But if you've got those things, the guts to color outside the lines and the smarts to know when it's worth the risk, you've got a shot at achieving something truly extraordinary.

So don't be afraid to break a few rules along the way. Don't be afraid to zig when everyone else zags. In the end, it's not the rule-followers who change the game - it's the rule-breakers. The ones who are willing to take the road less traveled, to blaze their own trail, no matter how unconventional it might seem.

Chapter Eight

Relationships and Networking

T he quality of our relationships and networks can either catapult us toward our goals or hold us back.

Law 35: Command respect

Commanding respect isn't about flexing or trying to intimidate people. It's about understanding the deep-rooted, subconscious factors that shape how humans perceive and respond to each other. In the business world, being seen as strong, capable, and reliable can give you a major leg up. It can make it easier to build alliances, lead teams and convince customers or investors to bet on you.

But this law isn't just about business strategy. It's about recognizing that taking care of yourself, both mentally and physically, is a crucial part of being successful. The path to becoming a respected figure in your field isn't just about what you know or what skills you have. It's also about nurturing your body and mind - the very tools you rely on to navigate the challenges of entrepreneurship and life itself.

Think about it like this: if you saw two people pitching the same business idea and one of them looked like they just rolled out of bed while the other looked sharp, fit and put together, who would you be more inclined to trust? It's not about superficiality - it's about the message you're sending about your ability to handle life.

When you prioritize your physical health and presentation, you're communicating a host of positive qualities without even opening your mouth. You're showing that you're disciplined, that you follow through, that you hold yourself to high standards. These are the kinds of traits that inspire confidence and respect in others.

Now, I'm not saying you need to become a bodybuilder or a fashion model to succeed in business. But I am saying that investing in your physical presence, in the way you carry yourself and present yourself to the world, can pay huge dividends. It can open doors, influence negotiations and give you that extra edge in a competitive landscape.

Law 36. Image sells

Your image is everything. It's not just about looking good - it's about the whole package. The way you present yourself, the way you carry yourself, the way you're perceived in the market. That's what "image sells" is all about.

Your image is like a billboard for your brand. It's broadcasting a message 24/7, whether you're aware of it or not. And that message can either be working for you or against you. If you're putting out an image of success, competence and reliability, people are gonna be lining up to do business with you. But if your image is sloppy, unprofessional, or inconsistent, you're shooting yourself in the foot before you even get started.

Now, when we talk about investing in your image, we're not just talking about wearing designer suits or driving a fancy car. I mean, those things can certainly help, but it's bigger than that. It's about the total package - how you groom yourself, how you communicate, how you show up in the world. It's about the quality of your website, your social media presence, your marketing materials. Every touchpoint is an opportunity to reinforce your brand and the value you provide.

And here's the thing - people are always gonna form an impression of you, whether you like it or not. It's human nature. We're visual creatures, and we make snap judgments based on what we see. So you might as well take control of that narrative. By crafting a strong, positive image, you're setting the stage for success before you even open your mouth.

But "image sells" isn't just about appearances. It's about the substance behind the style. When you present a polished, professional image, you're communicating a host of positive attributes. You're showing that you pay attention to detail, that you value quality, that you have self-respect. These are the kinds of things that resonate with people on a deep level. They make people want to associate with you, to do business with you, to be part of your tribe.

Ultimately, your image is a reflection of your personal brand. It's the unique combination of your skills, your personality and the value you bring to the table. And in today's hyper-competitive market, a strong personal brand can be your greatest asset. It can help you stand out, command higher prices, and build a loyal following.

So don't sleep on the power of image. Invest in yourself, in your presentation, in the way you show up in the world. Because when you do, you're not just selling a product or a service. You're selling a promise, a feeling, an experience.

Law 37: Speaking skills are essential

Being able to speak well is like having a cheat code for success. It's not just about what you say, but how you say it. Every time you open your mouth, whether it's in a meeting, a presentation, or just a casual conversation, you have a chance to make an impression. To show people a little bit of who you are, what you stand for and why they should give a damn.

Nobody wants to listen to a boring, monotone robot. The key to speaking well is to be engaging, to be authentic, to make people feel something. You gotta tell stories that stick in people's minds, that make them nod along and think, "Damn, this person knows what they're talking about." When you can do that, even an average idea can become a game-changer.

But here's the thing - you don't become a great speaker overnight. It's a skill, just like anything else. And like any skill, it takes practice. You gotta seek out opportunities to speak, to put yourself out there. Maybe it's speaking up more in meetings, or volunteering to give presentations. Hell, you could start a podcast or a YouTube channel. The point is, the more you do it, the more comfortable you'll get, and the better you'll become.

Now, I know we all have those moments where we're trying to get our point across and we start spitting out "umms" and "ahhs". But cut it out. When you eliminate those filler words, you instantly sound more confident, more in control. And that keeps people hanging on your every word.

But don't think you have to be talking non-stop. Sometimes, a well-placed pause can be just as powerful as the words you say. If you need a moment to gather your thoughts, take it. Let the silence do some of the heavy lifting for you.

At the end of the day, speaking well is about connecting with people. It's about making them feel heard, understood and inspired. When you can do that, you're not just a better communicator - you're a force to be reckoned with. In business and in life.

Law 38: Ditch Time Wasters

Your time is the most valuable thing you've got. More precious than any amount of cash, any shiny object you could buy. And if you want to make it in this world, to build something that matters, you gotta guard your time like a watchdog.

Time wasters, man. They're everywhere. And they come in all shapes and sizes. The negative Nancys who are always bitching about something, always trying to drag you down to their level. They don't believe in your vision, they don't support your dreams, and they sure as hell don't deserve a single second more of your time.

Look, I get it. Cutting these people out of your life, isn't easy. It can be uncomfortable, even painful at times. But you gotta think big picture here. Every minute you waste on something or someone that isn't pushing you towards your goals, that's a minute you're never gonna get back. And when you're trying to build your dream life, you can't afford to waste a single second.

So yeah, you might have to make some tough calls. You might have to distance yourself from certain people, certain habits. And yeah, you might hear some whispers. "Oh, look who thinks they're too good for us now." Fuck them. Those aren't insults, they're compliments. They're proof that you're evolving, that you're outgrowing the bullshit and focusing on what really matters.

Because here's the thing - real success, isn't about comfort. It's not about taking the easy road. It's about making the hard choices, the ones that might not feel good in the moment but will pay off big time down the line. It's about prioritizing your future over your present, your ambition over your complacency.

So start being ruthless with your time. Start cutting out the fat, the distractions, the energy vampires. Start surrounding yourself with people and activities that push you forward, that challenge you to be better. Because every second you spend on something worthwhile, is a second invested into your future. And trust me, those seconds add up.

Law 39: Surround yourself with winners

The people you surround yourself with have a profound impact on your life, both personally and professionally. The idea of surrounding yourself with winners isn't about being elitist or superficial - it's about recognizing the power of influence and using it to your advantage.

Winners, in this context, are those who share your values, your drive and your commitment to growth. They're the people who inspire you to be better, who challenge you to push past your limits and who support you through the ups and downs of your journey.

When you surround yourself with these kinds of people, you create an environment that's conducive to success. You're exposed to new ideas, new perspectives and new opportunities. You have a built-in support system of individuals who understand your goals and are invested in helping you achieve them.

On the flip side, surrounding yourself with people who are negative, complacent, or unmotivated can have a real dampening effect on your own ambitions. It's not about judging these people or thinking you're better than them - it's about recognizing that their energy and outlook can rub off on you, often in subtle ways.

Making a conscious effort to surround yourself with winners isn't always easy. It can mean making tough decisions about who you spend your time with and it can require you to step out of your comfort zone to forge new connections. But the payoff is immense.

By aligning yourself with people who are driven, positive and successful, you set yourself up to absorb those same qualities. You learn from their experiences, you're inspired by their achievements, and you're motivated to rise to their level.

In today's hyper-connected world, you have more opportunities than ever to find and connect with these kinds of people. Through social media, professional networks and even virtual events, you can tap into communities of like-minded individuals who can help you grow and thrive.

Before we go into the final section on mindset, I've put together a short bonus PDF called **The Millionaire Mindset Cheat Sheet**. It's a written breakdown of the core mindset principles from this book so you can revisit them faster and integrate them into your daily decisions.

the
MILLIONAIRE
MINDSET
cheatsheet

GRAB IT HERE

Chapter Nine

Mindset Principles

Law 40: Politics is a distraction

If you're trying to build real wealth, to create a business that's gonna stand the test of time, you can't get caught up in the political circus. It's truly just a distraction, a black hole that'll suck you in and spit you out with nothing to show for it.

I see so many people getting wrapped up in the daily drama of politics, spending hours arguing on social media or getting worked up over the latest headline. But here's the thing - none of that is gonna make or break your business. Your success depends on you - your actions, your strategies, your ability to adapt and innovate.

Sure, maybe taxes go up a bit under the new administration. Maybe there's some new trade policy that shakes things up. But at the end of the day, those things are just minor bumps in the road. If your business is solid, if you've built it on a foundation of smart decisions and hard work, you'll weather those changes just fine.

But if you're wasting your energy on political bullshit, letting that stuff consume your attention and your passion, you're taking your eye off the ball. You're not focusing on the things that really matter - like streamlining your operations, finding new growth opportunities, or sharpening your financial know-how.

Now, don't get me wrong. There may come a point where politics does start to matter for your business. When you've scaled to a certain level, when you're playing in the big leagues, then yeah - policy decisions can have a real impact on your bottom line. And at that point, you might have the clout to actually influence those decisions.

But until then? It's just a sideshow, man. It's just another shiny object trying to pull your focus away from what really counts.

So my advice? Tune out the noise. Don't get sucked into the never-ending debate. Keep your head down, keep grinding and keep building your empire. The politicos can duke it out all they want - but at the end of the day, it's the hustlers and the innovators who are gonna come out on top.

Law 41: Mix business with pleasure

You gotta learn to mix business with pleasure. You gotta turn every aspect of your life into an opportunity for growth and expansion.

Most people, have this idea that work and play are two separate things. They clock in, grind for eight hours, then clock out and try to enjoy whatever's left of their day. But that's a sucker's game. If you want to be successful, to be a real player, you gotta blur those lines.

Every dinner, every vacation, every party - aren't just chances to kick back and relax. They're opportunities to network, to scout new prospects, to plant the seeds of future deals. You need to approach every interaction with a strategic mindset, always thinking about how you can leverage it for your business.

Now, some people might hear this and think it sounds exhausting. Like you're never really "off the clock." But, that's the beauty of it - when you mix business with pleasure, when you align your passions with your professions, it doesn't feel like work anymore. It just feels like living life to the fullest.

Imagine you're on a beach vacation, sipping a cocktail and soaking up the sun. But while everyone else is zoning out, you're scanning the shoreline for potential real estate investments. Or you're at a birthday party, celebrating with friends, but you're also scoping out the room for possible collaborators or clients.

This is what it means to be relentless in your pursuit of success. It's about seizing every moment, turning every interaction into a potential win for your business. And the best part? When you live like this, when you make your hustle a natural part of your lifestyle, it doesn't drain you - it energizes you.

Of course, this doesn't mean you should be all business, all the time. You still need balance, still need time to recharge and reconnect with what matters. But by blurring the lines between work and play, and bringing a touch of pleasure to your business pursuits, you make the journey a whole lot more enjoyable.

So start looking at your life through this lens. Start seeing every social engagement, every hobby, every vacation as a chance to push your business forward. It might take some practice, might feel a little unnatural at first. But trust me - once you get a taste of the success this mindset can bring, you'll never go back.

Law 42: Stay resilient

You gotta be like an oak tree, man. Sturdy, deep-rooted, able to weather any storm that comes your way.

The thing about success is, it's not just about reaching the top. It's about surviving all the shit that gets thrown at you on the way up. Taking those punches, learning from them and coming back stronger every time.

When you're first starting out, it's gonna be tough. You're gonna face challenges that test you to your core, that make you question if you have what it takes. But that struggle is where you forge your steel. That's where you build the resilience that's gonna carry you through.

Once you make it through those early days, once you hit that first big milestone, it gets easier. Not easy, mind you. But easier. Because now you've got experience under your belt. You've seen some shit and you know how to handle it.

But the challenges, they don't stop coming. They just change. Maybe it's not about scraping together enough cash to keep the lights on anymore. Maybe now it's about navigating complex legal issues or managing a rapidly growing team. But because you've built that foundation of resilience, because you've been through the fire before, you're ready. You can adapt, you can overcome, you can keep pushing forward.

And that's the secret, really. That's what separates the one-hit wonders from the true icons. It's not just about having a great idea or a clever strategy. It's about having the grit, the determination, the sheer will to keep going, no matter what gets thrown your way.

When you have that resilience, that unshakable core, there's nothing that can stop you. Setbacks become springboards. Failures become lessons. And every challenge overcome just adds more fuel to your fire, propelling you to heights you never thought possible.

So embrace the struggle. Embrace the hardship. Don't shy away from the tough times - lean into them. Because it's in those moments, when you're pushed to your limits and beyond, that you'll find the strength you never knew you had.

And when you come out the other side, when you've weathered the storms and emerged victorious, you'll look back on those early days with a sense of pride. Because you didn't just survive - you thrived.

You took whatever life threw at you and used it to build something incredible.

Law 43: Sharpen your Sword

Your abilities, your strategies, your techniques - are your sword. And like any weapon, it needs constant care and attention to stay sharp.

It doesn't matter how good you are at what you do. It doesn't matter how many deals you've closed, how many successful campaigns you've run. If you're not constantly honing your craft, you're falling behind. Because in business, change isn't just a possibility - it's a guarantee.

New technologies emerge, consumer habits shift, markets evolve. And if you're not adapting, not staying on the cutting edge, you're gonna get left in the dust. That's why you gotta treat every day like a training session. Every interaction, every project, every challenge - is an opportunity to get better, to sharpen your sword.

Maybe that means taking a deep dive into the latest social media algorithms, figuring out how to optimize your content for maximum reach. Maybe it means studying the masters of persuasion, learning how to craft a sales pitch that's impossible to resist. Or maybe it's about getting your hands dirty with data, using analytics to uncover new insights and opportunities.

The point is, you can't ever stop learning. You can't ever stop pushing yourself to be better. Because the moment you get complacent, the moment you start resting on your laurels, that's when you become vulnerable. That's when some hungry young upstart comes along and eats your lunch.

But when you're always on the lookout for new ways to innovate, to optimize, to dominate. That's when you become unstoppable. That's when you can cut through the noise and the competition like a hot knife through butter.

This isn't just about staying relevant. It's not just about defending your turf. When you're always honing your skills, you're not just reacting to change - you're driving it. You're spotting opportunities before anyone else, seizing them while others are still playing catch-up.

So never stop sharpening. Never stop pushing. Treat every day like a chance to get better, to get faster, to get deadlier. Because in this game, it's not the biggest or the strongest who win. It's the sharpest.

Law 44: Irrational confidence

You have to believe in yourself and your abilities with a level of conviction that borders on delusional.

Now, I know what you're thinking. "Isn't that just being cocky? Isn't that setting myself up for disappointment?" But, that's where most people get it confused. Irrational confidence isn't about being arrogant or out of touch with reality. It's about having such a deep, unshakable faith in what you bring to the table that it becomes contagious.

When you radiate that kind of confidence, when you carry yourself with that level of self-assurance, people can't help but be drawn to you. Clients, partners, investors - they want to work with someone who believes in themselves and their vision with every fiber of their being.

Think about it. When you're pitching a project, negotiating a deal, rallying your team - do you want to come across as unsure, as hesitant? Hell no. You want to exude the confidence of someone who's been there, done that and has the trophy case to prove it.

But here's the key - this confidence, has to be real. It's gotta be rooted in a genuine belief in your skills, your knowledge, your value. It can't just be empty bravado or baseless boasting. People can smell that kind of bullshit from a mile away and it'll torpedo your credibility.

No, true irrational confidence comes from a place of deep self-awareness and self-assurance. It's about knowing exactly what you bring to the table and being unapologetic about it. It's about walking into every room, every interaction, with the unshakable conviction that you are the best at what you do.

And when you master that, when you can project that level of confidence with every word and every action, it becomes a self-fulfilling prophecy. Doubts melt away, objections vanish and people line up to be a part of whatever it is you're building.

But it's not just about winning over others. Irrational confidence is also about how you face challenges, how you bounce back from setbacks. When you truly believe in yourself and your abilities, there's no obstacle too big, no failure too daunting. You know that every stumble is just a stepping stone, every "no" just a redirection to a bigger "yes."

So cultivate that confidence. Nurture it, feed it, let it grow until it becomes an unshakable part of who you are. And then wear it like armor, let it shine through in every pitch, every handshake, every bold move you make.

Because in a world full of doubt and uncertainty, irrational confidence is the ultimate competitive edge. It's the x-factor that separates the contenders from the pretenders.

So believe in yourself, even when others don't. Back yourself, even when the odds seem stacked against you. And never, ever let anyone or anything shake your faith in what you're capable of.

Law 45: Seek out chaos

Learn to love chaos. Don't see it as a threat, but as an opportunity in disguise.

Most people panic when shit hits the fan. They freeze up, they run for cover, they pray for things to go back to normal. But not you. Not the real players in this game. When chaos comes knocking, you open the door with a grin on your face.

Because you know that it's in times of upheaval, in moments of disruption, that the biggest opportunities present themselves. It's when the status quo gets shaken up that new markets emerge, new solutions become possible, new fortunes are made.

Think about it. When an industry is in crisis, when everything's going to hell in a hand-basket, what do most companies do? They retrench. They play it safe, they cut costs, they try to ride out the storm. But while they're busy battening down the hatches, you know what you're doing? You're innovating. You're pivoting. You're finding ways to turn that chaos into cold, hard cash.

Maybe that means developing a product that addresses a sudden, pressing need. Maybe it means swooping in and scooping up assets that others are too scared to touch. Or maybe it just means being more agile, more responsive, more willing to take risks than your competitors.

The point is, chaos isn't something to be avoided. It's something to be embraced, something to be leveraged. Because it's in the midst of chaos that true greatness is forged. It's where leaders are made, where empires are built.

But to do that, to seize those opportunities, you have to have a mindset that's wired for hustle. To see past the immediate shitstorm and envision the possibilities that lie beyond. You gotta be willing to charge headfirst into the fray, to take bold action while others are still trying to find their footing.

It's not always easy. Chaos can be scary, it can be disorienting, it can make you question everything you thought you knew. But that's part of the game. That's the price of admission for the kind of success most people only dream about.

Seek out chaos. Embrace it, harness it, turn it into your greatest asset. While others are running scared, you'll be running laps around them. While they're trying to weather the storm, you'll be the one steering the ship.

Law 46: Vanishing Value Rule

Every 24 hours that pass without you pushing your goals forward, is cash that's slipping right through your fingers, never to be seen again.

I call this the Vanishing Value Rule. It's the idea that time is the most precious resource you have, and every moment you waste, every opportunity you let pass by, that's value that's disappearing into thin air. It's like a hotel with empty rooms - that's revenue they can never get back, no matter how booked up they are the next day.

And the same goes for you. When you're not making moves and seizing opportunities, that's potential profit that's vanishing before your very eyes. And here's the kicker - you can't make it up later. You can't hit pause on your journey to success and then just hit double speed to catch up. It doesn't work like that.

Every day is a fresh start, a new chance to get out there and make shit happen. But it's also a ticking clock, a reminder that if you don't grab life by the horns and make the most of every moment, those moments are gone forever.

That's why urgency is so important. That's why the most successful people in the world, don't hesitate. They don't second-guess themselves, they don't wait for the perfect moment. They take action, they make decisions, they keep pushing forward, day in and day out.

Because they know that success isn't something you can put off until tomorrow. It's not something you can just pencil into your schedule for next week or next month. It's something you have to chase down every single day, with everything you've got.

There will be days when you're tired, when you're discouraged, when you just want to take a break. But that's when the Vanishing Value Rule becomes more important than ever. That's when you have to remind yourself that every day counts, that every moment is an opportunity to get one step closer to your dreams.

So don't let those moments slip away. Don't let that value vanish into the ether. Wake up every morning ready to seize the day, ready to make your mark. And when your head hits the pillow at night, make sure you can look back and say, "I gave it my all. I made progress. I didn't let a single opportunity go to waste."

Law 47: Dopamine is your Friend

In this digital age, your phone isn't just some toy for killing time. It's a powerhouse, a tool that can either make or break you. And the key to making it work for you? Dopamine.

When most people pick up their phone, they're just looking for a quick hit. A little social media fix, a mindless game to pass the time. But that's small-time thinking. That's the mentality of a consumer, not a creator.

You have to flip the script. You need to start seeing your phone as a money-making machine, not a tool for distraction. Every time you pick it up, every notification you get, is an opportunity to hustle, to create, to build.

Maybe that means using social media to promote your brand, to engage with your audience, to build a following that's ride-or-die. Maybe it means leveraging online networks to connect with other hustlers, to find new opportunities, to make deals that'll take your business to the next level.

Or maybe it's about creating content, about putting your ideas and your talents out there for the world to see. Whether it's a video, a tweet, or a blog post that goes viral, every piece of content you create is a chance to make your mark, to attract new fans, new clients, new revenue streams.

When you start using your phone like this, seeing it as a tool for creation and not just consumption, something amazing happens. Those little dopamine hits, those little bursts of satisfaction you get from a like or a follow or a share, start adding up.

But it's not just about the short-term buzz. It's about the long-term payoff. Because every action you take on your phone, every move you make to grow your brand and your business, is a step towards the life you want. It's a step towards financial freedom, calling your own shots and being the kind of person who makes money in their sleep.

And the more you do it, the more you train your brain to associate your phone with hustling, with creating, with making shit happen, the easier it becomes. Suddenly, reaching for your phone isn't about zoning out - it's about tuning in, about seizing every opportunity to level up.

So don't be afraid to let dopamine be your friend. Don't be afraid to get hooked on the rush of making moves and making money. Because in this game, addiction isn't a weakness - it's a superpower.

Law 48: Time is NOT money

Most people get stuck in this 9-5 mindset. They think the only way to make more cash is to put in more hours, to grind harder, to hustle longer. But that's a sucker's game. Because no matter how much you earn per hour, there's always gonna be a limit to how many hours you can work.

But when you start thinking like an entrepreneur, when you start focusing on building systems and assets that can make money for you even when you're not working, that's when the game changes. That's when you break free from the constraints of trading time for dollars and tap into the true power of exponential growth.

Maybe that means creating a digital product that you can sell over and over again, without having to create it from scratch each time.

Maybe it means investing in real estate or stocks that appreciate in value and kick off passive income. Or maybe it means building a team or a network that can keep your business running and growing even when you're not there to manage every little detail.

The point is, when you start thinking in terms of systems and scalability, when you start looking for ways to make your money work for you instead of the other way around, you open up a whole new world of possibilities. You're no longer limited by the number of hours in a day or the amount of effort you can put in personally.

This isn't just about working smarter instead of harder (although that's definitely part of it). It's about a fundamental shift in mindset. It's about evolving from a worker bee mentality to a visionary entrepreneur mentality.

Because when you're just trading time for money, you're always gonna be stuck on that hamster wheel. No matter how much you earn per hour, you're still just another cog in someone else's machine. But when you start building your own machines, when you start creating platforms and systems that can generate wealth on autopilot, that's when you become the one in control.

And yeah, it's not always easy. It takes a lot of hard work and smart strategies to get to that point. But the payoff is more than worth it. Because when you detach your financial success from the constraints of time, when you create income streams that can flow whether you're working or not, you unlock a level of freedom and abundance that makes life worth living.

So never forget. Time is precious, but it's not the same thing as money. Money is something you can create, something you can multiply, something you can make work for you. Time is the canvas you have to work with.

Use that canvas wisely. Build systems, invest in assets, create platforms that can scale and grow beyond the limits of your own effort. And always, always be looking for ways to delink your income from your hours.

Chapter Ten

Conclusion

Alright, you've made it to the end. By now, you have a solid grasp on the mindset and strategies needed to stack some serious cash and build your dream life. But here's the thing - that's just the beginning.

Too many read a book like this, get all hyped up, and then go right back to their same old bullshit cycle. They stay stuck in the 9-5 grind, trading their precious time for scraps, always dreaming about the life they want but never making any real moves to get it.

But I know that isn't you. You're going to be different.

You're sick of watching others build their dreams while you're stuck. You're tired of having brilliant ideas but no clue how to make them real. You're done with dreaming about freedom while your bank account keeps you chained to mediocrity.

Remember to stay hungry, stay ruthless, and never forget - your mind is the key to the vault. Master it and there's no limit to what you can achieve.

Before you head out and start crushing it, please do me a solid and leave a quick rating of the book. Let me know which laws hit you hardest, which ones you're gonna put into action first and how you're gonna use them to build your empire. Not only will your feedback help make this guide even better, but it also helps the book show up for other hungry hustlers like yourself.

Now go out there and show the world who you are!